'I will continue fighting for freedom until the end of my days'
(The Struggle is My Life press statement, 26 June 1961)

Through his words and deeds Nelson Mandela has been embraced by the whole world as a symbol of courage, hope and reconciliation.

Collected in this volume, his comments on subjects as diverse as Humanity, Racism, Friendship, Oppression and Freedom provide an insight into the man and all he stands for.

By turns moving, generous, humorous and sad, *In the words of Nelson Mandela* eloquently conveys his warmth and dignity. It will be both an inspiration and source of strength for all who read it.

Jennifer Crwys-Williams is a South African journalist and broadcaster.

In the words of
Nelson Mandela

A Little Pocketbook

Edited by Jennifer Crwys-Williams

PENGUIN BOOKS

PENGUIN BOOKS

Published by the Penguin Group
Penguin Books (South Africa) (Pty) Ltd, 24 Sturdee Avenue, Rosebank,
Johannesburg 2196, South Africa
Penguin Books Ltd, 80 Strand, London WC2R 0RL, England
Penguin Group (USA) Inc, 375 Hudson Street, New York, New York
10014, USA
Penguin Group (Canada), 90 Eglinton Avenue East, Suite 700, Toronto,
Ontario, Canada M4P 2Y3 (a division of Pearson Penguin Canada Inc)
Penguin Ireland, 25 St Stephen's Green, Dublin 2, Ireland (a division of
Penguin Books Ltd)
Penguin Group (Australia), 250 Camberwell Road, Camberwell, Victoria
3124, Australia (a division of Pearson Australia Group Pty Ltd)
Penguin Books India Pvt Ltd, 11 Community Centre, Panchsheel Park,
New Delhi – 110 017, India
Penguin Group (NZ), Cnr Rosedale and Airborne Roads, Albany, Auckland
1310, New Zealand (a division of Pearson New Zealand Ltd)

Penguin Books (South Africa) (Pty) Ltd, Registered Offices:
24 Sturdee Avenue, Rosebank, Johannesburg 2196, South Africa

www.penguinbooks.co.za

First published by Penguin Books (South Africa) (Pty) Ltd 1997
This edition published 2004
Reprinted 2008

Copyright © Jennifer Crwys-Williams 1997

ISBN 978-0-140-27049-5

Typeset by CJH Design in 11 on 13 pt Joanna
Printed and bound by Formeset Printers, Cape Town

Printed on Sappi Avalon Supreme Matt 135g/m^2

This book is dedicated to the children of South Africa in the hope that as they grow they may find inspiration from the thoughts of Nelson Rolihlahla Mandela – and that, in his words on receiving the Nobel Peace Prize, they and other children the world over, may 'play in the open veld, no longer tortured by the pangs of hunger or ravaged by disease or threatened with the scourge of ignorance, molestation and abuse . . . Children are the greatest of our treasures.'

In particular, I hope this little book inspires the children in my own family, living in both the old and the new worlds: Amber, Cassandra, Sebastian, Phoebe and Blaise.

Acknowledgements

My special thanks to the journalists who, over the years, have interviewed Nelson Mandela and who have provided me with much of the material used in this book.

I received substantial amounts of help for the first edition of this book from Susan Segar, then political correspondent of *The Natal Witness*. Thanks, again, to my agent, Carole Blake of Blake Friedmann & Associates.

Introduction

Known to his countrymen and women as
Madiba, Nelson Mandela is the world's role
model. A towering figure of strength and forgive-
ness, during the brief years of his presidency he
was able to do the almost impossible: help unite
the bitterly divided people of the country of his
birth, South Africa. In so doing, he has been
taken to the heart of both the mighty and the
dispossessed the world over.

Whilst remaining a South African to the last fibre
of his being, Nelson Mandela now belongs to
everyone, irrespective of where they live and,
importantly for him, how they live. He has
become, since his release from twenty-seven
years of imprisonment, a symbol of reconciliation
and, in a world divided by sectarian hatreds, a
symbol of love.

He would protest; he avers that he is no saint –
but to South Africans, Nelson Mandela's
squabbling rainbow people, he has, quite
simply, no parallel.

Perhaps his thoughts, reproduced on these

pages, and honed over many years of tribulation, will inspire people, young and old, moneyed and impoverished, the world over. In particular, I hope it will inspire people who have had few role models in their lives, and who have suffered their own apartheids in their own countries.

Jennifer Crwys-Williams

On Abortion

Women have the right to decide what they want to do with their bodies.

On His Achievements

Don't tempt me to beat my chest and to say this is what I have done!

In spite of interviewers the world over hoping for intimate revelations, Nelson Mandela dislikes speaking about himself and invariably refers to the 'collective' – meaning, of course, the African National Congress.

I must not be isolated from the collective who are responsible for the success.

When I make a mistake, I normally say: 'It's these young chaps,' and when they do something good, I say: 'This is the man.'

To illustrate his point, Madiba beat his chest – this was in an internationally televised interview, December 1997: Mandela Meets the Media.

On Africa

For centuries, an ancient continent has bled from many gaping sword wounds.

No doubt Africa's renaissance is at hand – and our challenge is to steer the continent through the tide of history.

The people of the continent are eager and willing to be among the very best in all areas of endeavour.

The peoples of resurgent Africa are perfectly capable of deciding upon their own future form of government and discovering and themselves dealing with any dangers which might arise.

We need to exert ourselves that much more, and break out of the vicious cycle of dependence imposed on us by the financially powerful; those in command of immense market power and those who dare to fashion the world in their own image.

Africa, more than any other continent, has had to contend with the consequences of conquest in a denial of its own role in history, including the denial that its people had the capacity to bring about change and progress.

It would be a cruel irony of history if Africa's actions to regenerate the continent were to unleash a new scramble for Africa which, like that of the nineteenth century, plundered the continent's wealth and left it once more the poorer.

Conflict threatens not only the gains we have made but also our collective future.

The African rebirth is now more than an idea – its seeds are being sown in the regional communities we are busy building and in the continent as a whole.

Can we continue to tolerate our ancestors being shown as people locked in time?

Africa yearns and deserves to redeem her glory, to reassert her centuries-old contribution to economics, politics, culture and the arts; and once more to be a pioneer in the many fields of human endeavour.

One destabilising conflict anywhere on the continent is one too many.

For as long as the majority of people anywhere on the continent feel oppressed, are not allowed democratic participation in decision-making processes, and cannot elect their own leaders in free and fair elections, there will always be tension and conflict.

A continent which, while it led in the very evolution of human life and was a leading centre of learning, technology and the arts in ancient times, has experienced various traumatic epochs, each one of which has pushed her peoples deeper into poverty and backwardness.

We cannot abuse the concept of national sovereignty to deny the rest of the Continent the right and duty to intervene when, behind those sovereign boundaries, people are being slaughtered to protect tyranny.

He said this in June 1998 in his address to the Organization of African Unity.

We should treat the question of peace and stability on our continent as a common challenge.

On Being an African

Teach the children that Africans are not one iota inferior to Europeans.

From his seminal 'No Easy Walk to Freedom' address, 21 August 1953.

The lack of human dignity experienced by Africans is the direct result of the policy of white supremacy.

Spoken from the dock at the Rivonia Treason Trial, 20 April 1964, which sent him to prison for twenty-seven long years.

All of us, descendants of Africa, know only too well that racism demeans the victims and dehumanizes its perpetrators.

We are rising from the ashes of war.

He said this while presenting the Africa Peace Award to the war-torn country of Mozambique in November 1997. Madiba's wife, Graça Machel, is the widow of the former president of that country and he feels a great bond with it.

On the African National Congress

As no man is an island, so too are we not men of stone who are unmoved by the noble passions of love, friendship and human compassion.

He was referring to the formation of the ANC Youth League on Easter Sunday, 1944. Mandela and his lifelong friends Oliver Tambo and Walter

Sisulu, were prominent among its founding fathers – the young Turks of their day. This quotation was from a speech made in Uppsala Cathedral, Sweden, in March 1990.

We must move from the position of a resistance movement to one of builders.

For us the struggle against racism has assumed the proportions of a crusade.

The African National Congress is the greatest achievement of the twentieth century.

From an interview in 1997, the year he relinquished his presidency of the party.

I have always been a member of the African National Congress and I will remain a member of the African National Congress until I die.

On the African Renaissance

As we dream and work for the regeneration of our continent, we remain conscious that the African Renaissance can only succeed as part of the development of a new and equitable world order in which all the formerly colonised and marginalised take their rightful place, makers of history rather than the possessions of others.

As we stand on the threshold of a new African era characterised by democracy, sustainable economic development and a reawakening of our rich cultural values and heritage, African unity remains our watchword and the Organization of African Unity our guide.

On Afrikaners

As those who drew benefits from a previous programme of affirmative action, they should realize better than anyone else how such a programme can contribute towards making the community more productive.

I have often noticed Afrikaans people remark that the new South Africa gives them a feeling of freedom now that they have entered a wider world of relationships with fellow South Africans.

The challenge of the New Patriotism is not one of a choice between Afrikanerdom and being South African. On the contrary, it is precisely about the healing reconciliation of Afrikaners with being fully South African.

Maybe it was out of fear that they themselves would one day become the oppressed once again.

On possible reasons for the Afrikaners oppressing fellow South Africans during apartheid, and spoken in the tense run-up to South Africa's first democratic election in 1994.

When an Afrikaner changes, he changes completely.

Many Afrikaners, who once acted with great cruelty and insensitivity towards the majority in our country, to an extent you have to go to jail to understand, have changed completely and become loyal South Africans in whom one can trust.

On Age

What nature has decreed should not generate undue insecurity.

I am nearing my end. I want to be able to sleep until eternity with a broad smile on my face, knowing that the youth, opinion-makers and everybody is stretched across the divide, trying to unite the nation.

From a speech to students at the University of Potchefstroom, February 1996. He was then seventy-seven. Nelson Mandela was born in the tiny Transkei village of Mvezo on 18 July 1918.

I will be eighty-one when I finally retire, and I never thought a man in his seventies should take over an organization like the ANC.

The autumn of our lives presages the African spring.

He said this in Ouagadougou, Burkina Faso, addressing the Organization of African Unity. He celebrated his eightieth birthday at home in Johannesburg with his family on 18 July 1998.

One of the advantages of old age is that people respect you because of your grey hair and say all manner of nice things about you that are not based on who you really are.

I only keep myself busy so that I can prove that although I'm a has-been, I've still got some work to do.

Said in 2002, when he was as busy as ever.

To be an old man is very nice because, as a young man, I didn't get the support I am getting now.

He recounted the $10 million given to him by TV talk-show host Oprah Winfrey, and a number of banks whom he phoned at intervals of 15 minutes, raising enough money to send 20 young people to university. The occasion was the launch in Johannesburg, July 2003, of the Mindset Network educational project. Nelson Mandela joked that the first thing he would do when he reached the 'next world' would be to ferret out the billionaires. 'I am going to say to them "raise money" because I know the poor are everywhere and these children need to go to school.'

On Aids

Aids is clearly a disaster, effectively wiping out the development gains of the past decades and sabotaging the future.

Nelson Mandela was closing the thirteenth International Aids Conference in Durban, July 2000, and drew a standing ovation.

The challenge is to move from rhetoric to action, and action at an unprecedented intensity and scale.

There is no shame to disclose a terminal disease from which you are suffering.

He said this in 2002, after making a deliberate gesture by publicly embracing HIV-infected Aids activist Zackie Achmat; he also disclosed that three members of his own family had died of Aids. He was criticised by a prominent gay HIV-positive South African judge, Edwin Cameron, for failing to give a message on Aids when he was president. 'In 199 ways, he was our country's saviour. In the 200th way, he was not.'

Those who are infected with this terrible disease do not want stigma, they want love.

On the fifth anniversary of the death of Britain's Princess Diana (August 2002), he paid special tribute to her work in smashing the superstitions surrounding the disease. He noted that she had gone to hospitals with Aids patients, sitting on their beds and shaking hands. 'We have to continue to break that stigma,' he noted at the time.

It is a travesty of human rights on a global scale.

He was speaking in Paris in July 2003, and was referring to the prohibitive cost of anti-retroviral drugs for impoverished sufferers.

I was just a number. Millions of people today infected with Aids are classified as just a number. They too are serving a prison sentence for life.

Nelson Mandela launched his 46664 Give One Minute of Your Life to Aids campaign, in October 2003. The culmination of the campaign was the 46664 concert at Green Point Stadium, Cape Town, on 29 November 2003.

A tragedy of unprecedented proportions is unfolding in Africa.

This statement was a precursor to the 46664 concert for Aids. People worldwide were urged to phone 082 1 46664 to listen to music – and raise money for the fight against the dread disease.

Aids today in Africa is claiming more lives than the sum total of all wars, famines and floods and the ravages of such deadly diseases as malaria.

On Alliances

No true alliance can be built on the shifting
sands of evasions, illusions, and opportunism.

On Anger

Anger is a temporary feeling – you soon forget it,
particularly if you are involved in positive
activities and attitudes.

It is not easy to remain bitter if one is busy with
constructive things.

On Apartheid

Apartheid is the rule of the gun and the hangman.

The universal struggle against apartheid was not
an act of charity arising out of pity for our people,
but an affirmation of our common humanity.

Out of the experience of an extraordinary human
disaster that lasted too long, must be born a
society of which all humanity will be proud.

At his inauguration as President of South Africa, 10 May 1994.

It would have been immoral to keep quiet while a racist tyranny sought to reduce an entire people into a status worse than that of beasts of the forest.

The millions of graves strewn across Europe which are the result of the tyranny of Nazism, the decimation of the native peoples of the Americas and Australia, the destructive trail of the apartheid regime against humanity – all these are like a haunting question that floats in the wind: why did we allow these to happen?

Apartheid continues to live with us in the leaking roofs and corrugated walls of shacks; in the bulging stomachs of hungry children; in the darkness of homes without electricity; and in the heavy pails of dirty water that rural women carry for long distances to cook and to quench their thirst.

He said this in November 1997, one month before stepping down as president of the ANC.

At each turn of history, apartheid was bound to spawn resistance; it was destined to bring to life the forces that would guarantee its death.

With the exception of the atrocities against the Jews during World War II, there is no evil that has been as condemned by the entire world as apartheid.

He was speaking in December 1998, his last full year as President of South Africa.

On a Bill of Rights

A Bill of Rights is an important statement about the nature of power relations in any society.

The ANC has had a Bill of Rights since 1923.

A Bill of Rights cannot be associated with the political or economic subordination of either the majority or the minority.

A Bill of Rights is a living thing.

On Black Consciousness

In various forms and under various labels, this attitude of mind and way of life have coursed through the veins of all the motive forces of struggle.

Black consciousness has fired the determination of leaders and the masses alike.

The driving thrust of black consciousness was to forge pride and unity amongst all the oppressed, to foil the strategy of divide-and-rule, to engender pride among the mass of our people and confidence in their ability to throw off their oppression.

Above all, the liberation movement asserted that the people would most readily develop consciousness of their proud being, of their equality with everyone else, of their capacity to make history.

The value that black consciousness placed on culture reverberated across our land; in our prisons; and amongst the communities in exile – and our people, who were once enjoined to look to Europe and America for creative sustenance, turned their eyes to Africa.

On South African Blacks

The blacks think this transformation was brought about by military victory, and they have defeated the whites. They think the whites are

lying on the floor and begging for mercy.
From an interview during his July 1996 state visit to Britain.

On His 80th Birthday

If you live until eighty you have the respect of everybody, including those who used to despise you.
Nelson Mandela celebrated his eightieth birthday at his home in Houghton, Johannesburg, South Africa, by quietly marrying Graça Machel, the former wife of the late President of Mozambique, Samora Machel. Their marriage delighted the world.

If I could be given another eighty years.
This was said in response to a journalist's question: What would you like for your birthday?

I have been quite overwhelmed by the expressions of good wishes. There is so much to be thankful for.

On Bosnia

They (the leaders) thought through their blood and not through their brains.

On Boxing

Any boxer with skill I admire.

I did not enjoy the violence of boxing as much as the science of it.

In the ring, rank, age, colour and wealth are irrelevant.

Nelson Mandela was a heavyweight boxer himself, training every evening at Jerry Moloi's boxing gymnasium, Soweto.

On Boycotts

By and large, boycotts are recognized and accepted by the people as an effective and powerful weapon of political struggle.

On the British

I regard the British parliament as the most democratic institution in the world, and the independence and impartiality of its judiciary never fail to arouse my admiration.

On Cairo

Africa's greatest city.

On Cape Town

It was here, three centuries ago, that sailors from Europe triggered off the chain of the dispossession whose consequences we are still grappling with today.

In Cape Town resides part of the souls of many nations and cultures, priceless threads in the rich diversity of our African nation.

The city hosted me and my colleagues for over twenty-six years.

Robben Island lies off the coast of Cape Town and can be clearly seen from Table Mountain. Cape Town, of course, was also the city which welcomed him on his first day of freedom.

On the Caribbean

(The Caribbean) has, in song and verse, in political philosophy and action, long been a source for the articulation of both the lamentations and aspirations of black people everywhere.

When Africans were wrenched from their continent, they carried Africa with them and made the Caribbean a part of Africa.

On Change

Belief in the possibility of change and renewal is perhaps one of the defining characteristics of politics and of religions.

On Charity

Cash handouts might sustain you for a few months, at the end of which your problems remain.

On His Childhood

When I was a boy brought up in my village in the Transkei, I listened to the elders of the tribe telling stories about the good old days, before the arrival of the white man.

In his autobiography, Long Walk to Freedom, *Mandela writes touchingly about his childhood. His collaborator on the book was* Time *contributor Richard Stengel; it took eighteen months to write, starting with a manuscript Mandela had begun secretly in his prison cell. They began work daily at 6.45 a.m. – Mandela is an early riser to this day.*

I hoped and vowed then that, among the treasures that life might offer me, would be the opportunity to serve my people and make my own humble contribution to the freedom struggle.

The elders would tell us about the liberation and how it was fought by our ancestors in defence of our country, as well as the acts of valour performed by generals and soldiers during those epic days.

On Children

Children are the most vulnerable citizens in any society and the greatest of our treasures.
Nobel Peace Prize ceremony, Oslo, Norway, 1993.

The children must, at last, play in the open veld, no longer tortured by the pangs of hunger or ravaged by disease or threatened with the scourge of ignorance, molestation and abuse, and no longer required to engage in deeds whose gravity exceeds the demands of their tender years.

The reward of the ending of apartheid will and must be measured by the happiness and welfare of the children.

The children who sleep in the streets, reduced to begging to make a living, are testimony to an unfinished job.

There can be no keener revelation of a society's soul than the way in which it treats its children.

Taken from his summary of the first year of the Nelson Mandela Children's Fund, 1996 (on the Worldwide Web at http://www.web.co.za/mandela/children).

The true character of a society is revealed in how it treats its children.

When you see the children, the way they are dressed, completely emaciated, you are really moved.

He was speaking about children in general, and about the children who live around the Transkei villages he calls home, in particular.

On Circumcision

The pain went into the marrow of my bones.

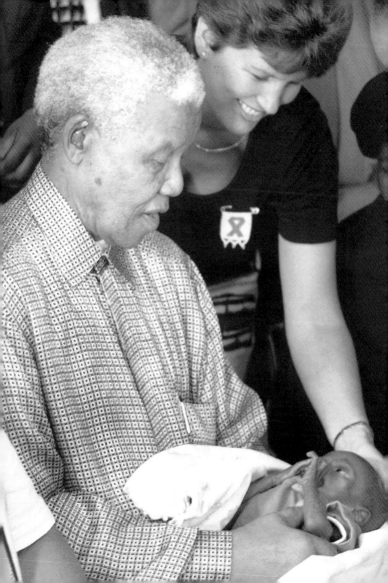

I was not as forthright and strong as the other boys that preceded me.

The fact that courage is expected of you in the face of the unbearable gives you strength for the rest of your life.

On Clothes

My father gave me his riding breeches and he cut them, and they had twine which I used as a belt, and that is how I went to school for the first time. I had a pair of shorts, sandals but no socks, a sleeveless shirt and no underwear, which is very humiliating.

Talking to the then editor of French Vogue, *December 1993, and referring to the early days of his imprisonment – a far cry from the 'Madiba style' shirts he has made famous. They are generally made of and lined with silk – and the pattern is perfectly aligned, making them costly in terms of fabric to make.*

There isn't a single article I wear that I have bought – people just generously give me clothes.

After seven months as President in 1994.

Every time I put on a bow tie I am so uncomfortable I can hardly talk.

Everybody just looks at my face – not at my clothes.

On Colonialism

The resistance of the black man to white colonial intrusion was crushed by the gun.

Taken from Mandela's letter, smuggled out of Robben Island after the 1976 Soweto uprising, and published internationally by the ANC in 1980.

The nineteenth-century colonization of the African continent was in many respects the culmination of the Renaissance-initiated expansion of European dominion over the planet.

On Communication

One of our strongest weapons is dialogue.

On Communism

For many decades communists were the only political group in South Africa who were prepared to treat Africans as human beings and their equals; who were prepared to eat with us; talk with us, live with us and work with us.

Spoken from the dock at the Rivonia Treason Trial, 20 April 1964.

There is so much hypocrisy behind some of this red-baiting that it sickens me, and I feel like saying to the culprits: 'How dare you say to me, a man of seventy-five, that I must denounce my friends, and for whom?'

On Compromise

That is the nature of compromising: you can compromise on fundamental issues.

At one of his first interviews after his release from twenty-seven years' imprisonment, 15 February 1990. He was released on 11 February 1990.

If you are not prepared to compromise, then you must not enter into or think about the process of negotiation at all.

Compromise must not undermine your own position.

Insignificant things, peripheral issues, don't need any compromise.

On Conciliation

No organization whose interests are identical with those of the toiling masses will advocate conciliation to win its demands.

On the Congressional Gold Medal, USA

The award with which you honour me is an expression of the common humanity that binds us one person to another, nation to nation, and people of the north to people of the south.

He received the medal at the Rotunda on Capitol Hill, Washington on 23 September 1998, his last visit to the USA as President of South Africa.

I receive it with pride, as a symbol of the partnership for peace, prosperity and equity as we enter the new millennium.

The medal has also been received by Mother Teresa, Winston Churchill, Thomas Edison, Walt Disney and Joe Louis among roughly 100 others.

On the South African Constitution

We give life to our nation's prayer for freedom regained and a continent reborn.

On signing the new South African constitution into law at Sharpeville, 10 December 1996.

Let us now, drawing strength from the unity which we have forged, together grasp the opportunities and realize the vision enshrined in this constitution.

Respect for human life, liberty and well-being must be enshrined as rights beyond the power of any force to diminish.

On Criticism

If the criticism is valid, is must be made.

On Culture

Like truth, culture and creativity are enduring.

On His Culture

In my culture we don't discuss personal
questions with young people.

Our families are far larger than those of whites
and it is always a pleasure to be fully accepted
throughout a village, district, or even several
districts, accompanied by your clan, and be a
beloved household member, where you can call
at any time, completely relaxed, sleep at ease
and freely take part in the discussion of all
problems, where you can even be given livestock
and land to build, free of charge.

From an undated letter to his cousin Sisi, written from Robben Island.

On the Dead

In eulogies to the departed, the works of the
living sometimes bear little relation to reality.

The names of only very few people are
remembered beyond their lives.

On His Death

It would be very egotistical of me to say how I would like to be remembered. I'd leave that entirely to South Africans. I would just like a simple stone on which is written, 'Mandela'.

Taken from a moving article for The New York Times *magazine by Anthony Lewis, 23 March 1997.*

There will be life after Mandela.

On the Death Sentence

The death sentence is a reflection of the animal instinct still in human beings.

On Democracy

What is important is not only to attain victory for democracy, it is to retain democracy.

Democracy and human rights are inseparable.

A democratic political order must be based on the majority principle, especially in a country where the vast majority have been systematically denied their rights.

On Demonstrations

Mass action is a peaceful form of channelling the anger of the people.

On Detention Without Trial

The detention without trial of political opponents is contrary to the basic principles of a democratic polity.

On Determination

As long as you have an iron will you can turn misfortune into advantage.

From a letter to his daughter, Zindzi Mandela, September 1990.

On Discipline

Discipline is the most powerful weapon to get liberation.

An organization can only carry out its mandate if there is discipline, and where there is no discipline there can be no real progress.

On Domesticity

I make my own bed every day. I don't allow the ladies who look after me to do it. I can cook a decent meal . . . I can polish a floor.

On Education

Parents have the right to choose the kind of education that shall be given to their children.

Make every home, every shack or rickety structure a centre of learning.

On Election Day (27-28 April 1994)

It was as though we were a nation reborn.
Nelson Mandela was seventy-five when he cast his first vote at Ohlange High School, Inanda, KwaZulu-Natal.

We can loudly proclaim from the rooftops – Free at last! Free at last!

After Martin Luther King, Jnr (the closing words from his 'I Have a Dream' speech, Washington DC, 28 August 1963). Nelson Mandela spoke the words on the first day of the first democratic South African elections, 27 April 1994.

I stand before you humbled by your courage with a heart full of love for all of you.

On Emigration

To this day we continue to lose some of the best among ourselves because the lights in the developed world shine brighter.

On Enemies

If a man fights back he is likely to get more respect than he would if he capitulated.

At his Bishopscourt, Cape Town, press conference on 15 February 1990, his first after his release from twenty-seven years' imprisonment.

I wanted South Africa to see that I loved even my enemies while I hated the system that turned us against one another.

Mandela's presidency was notable for the efforts he made towards reconciliation – including taking tea in the all-white Boer enclave of Oranje

with the widow of the architect of apartheid, Dr Hendrik Verwoerd, and
meeting Dr Percy Yutar, prosecuting attorney at the Rivonia Treason Trial.

On His Family

I have had to separate myself from my dear wife
and children, from my mother and sisters, to live
as an outlaw in my own land.

I am convinced that your pain and suffering was
far greater than my own.
Said during his first speech as a free man, at a rally in Cape Town, 11
February 1990.

I did not in the beginning choose to place my
people above my family, but in attempting to
serve my people, I found I was prevented from
fulfilling my obligations as a son, a brother, a
father and a husband.
He has said this frequently, and might have added 'and as a grandfather'.
In 1997 he had twenty-one grandchildren.

Our political activities have just destroyed our
family.
Spoken after two and a half years as President of South Africa and
referring, sadly, to his retirement, which he expected to be spent largely as a
global statesman.

To see your family, your children being persecuted when you are absolutely helpless in jail, that is one of the most bitter experiences, most painful experiences, I have had.

Playing with your grandchildren makes me forget about the troubles of the world.

On Favourite Things

My favourite animal is the impala because it is alert, curious, rapid and able to get out of difficult conditions easily – and with grace.

Taken from French Vogue, *December 1993/January 1994. It was a historic issue – edited by Nelson Mandela himself – and now a collector's item.*

Koeksisters are my favourite: in 1941 I was paid £2 a month and I reserved 10/- each weekend for koeksisters.

Koeksisters are a sticky Afrikaans sweet: plaited dough, deep fried and dunked in cold syrup. He was talking to satirist Pieter-Dirk Uys.

My favourite pastime: reading.

On Freedom

There is no easy walk to freedom.

He was thiry-five when he made that statement in his famous 'No Easy Walk to Freedom' speech. The words were originally spoken by India's first prime minister after independence, Jawaharlal Nehru.

Too many have suffered for the love of freedom.

Still imprisoned, this was from his first speech in almost twenty-five years. It was read in Johannesburg to wildly cheering crowds by his youngest daughter, Zindzi, on 10 February 1985.

Only free men can negotiate.

No power on earth can stop an oppressed people determined to win their freedom.

From 'The Struggle is My Life' press statement, 26 June 1961.

There is no such thing as part freedom.

Only through hardship, sacrifice and militant action can freedom be won.

No South African should rest and wallow in the joy of freedom.

To men, freedom in their own land is the pinnacle of their ambitions, from which nothing can turn men of conviction aside.

We do not want freedom without bread, nor do we want bread without freedom.

To overthrow oppression is the highest aspiration of every free man.

From Mandela's 'Black Man in a White Court' statement at his trial held in the Old Synagogue, Pretoria, from 15 October 1962 to 7 November 1962.

A man who takes away another man's freedom is a prisoner of hatred.

After twenty-seven years' imprisonment, Nelson Mandela walked to freedom through the gates of Victor Verster Prison, Paarl, at 4.16 p.m. on 11 February 1990. He was seventy-one.

Freedom cannot be achieved unless women have been emancipated from all forms of oppression.

To be free is not merely to cast off one's chains, but to live in a way that respects and enhances the lives of others.

Our freedom is incomplete without the freedom of the Palestinians; without the resolution of conflicts in East Timor, the Sudan and other parts of the world.

The choice is not between freedom and justice on the one hand, and their opposite, on the other.

For as long as legitimate bodies of opinion feel stifled, vile minds will take advantage of justifiable grievances to destroy, to kill and to maim.

On the Freedom Charter (1955)

It has received international acclaim as an outstanding human rights document.

The Charter is more than a mere list of demands for democratic reforms.

On Friendship

Friendship and support from friends is something which is a source of tremendous inspiration always and to everyone.

Those who are ready to join hands can overcome the greatest challenges.

On the Future

The fall of our century will carry away the foliage
of bitterness which has accumulated in our
hearts, and to which colonialism, neo-colonialism
and white minority domination gave birth.

On Goals

The ways in which we will achieve our goals are
bound by context, changing with circumstances
even while remaining steadfast in our
commitment to our vision.

On Government

When a government seeks to suppress a peaceful
demonstration of an unarmed people by
mobilizing the entire reserves of the state,
military and police, it concedes powerful mass
support for such a demonstration.

Said in 1961, when he was living in hiding and was referred to as the
Black Pimpernel in the nation's press. A small monument has now been

*erected close to the spot where he was finally arrested on the night of 5 July
1962 outside the small KwaZulu-Natal town of Howick.*

There is always a danger that when there is no
opposition, the governing party can become too
arrogant – too confident of itself.

There is nothing which makes people more
appreciative of a government than that it should
be able to deliver services.

On Government Corruption

Corruption in government – that is a plague that
must be erased from every regime in every place
in the world.

On Harlem, New York

Harlem symbolizes the strength and beauty in
resistance and you have taught us that out of
resistance to injustice comes renaissance,
renewal and rebirth.

On Health

The wounds that cannot be seen are more painful than those that can be treated by a doctor.

On Heroes

No single individual can assume the role of hero or Messiah.

There are men and women chosen to bring happiness into the hearts of people – those are the real heroes.

On His Heroes

Muhammed Ali was an inspiration to me even in prison because I thought of his courage and commitment. He used mind and body in unison and achieved success.

I would never miss a movie with Sophia Loren in it.

Kobie Coetsee – I have immense respect for that man because when no member of the National Party wanted to hear about the ANC, he was working systematically with me. He is one of my heroes.

Kobie Coetsee was Minister of Justice under P.W. Botha prior to Nelson Mandela's release on 11 February 1990.

My heroes are men and women, black and white, who are worried about socio-economic questions: people like Mother Teresa and many others — these are my heroes.

He said this in a television interview with talk-show host Tim Modise on Carte Blanche in July 2003. The interview, mostly done at Shambala game lodge, was in celebration of Nelson Mandela's eighty-fifth birthday.

On Himself

I have always regarded myself, in the first place, as an African patriot.

From the dock at the Rivonia Treason Trial, 20 April 1964. It took him two weeks, working in his cell at night, to write the speech.

I don't think there is much history can say about me.

I wanted to be able to stand and fight with my people and to share the hazards of war with them.

From the Rivonia Treason Trial, 20 April 1964.

I was made, by the law, a criminal, not because of what I had done, but because of what I stood for, because of what I thought, because of my conscience.

Spoken at the Old Synagogue Trial, Pretoria, 7 November 1962.

I'm an ordinary person, I have made serious mistakes, I have serious weaknesses.

I am what I am, both as a result of people who respected me and helped me, and of those who did not respect me and treated me badly.

I will pass through this world but once, and I do not want to divert my attention from my task, which is to unite the nation.

Spoken in February 1996 when he was seventy-seven years old.

Sometimes I feel like one who is on the sidelines, who has missed life itself.

Rather than being an asset, I'm more of a decoration.

Referring to himself as President of South Africa.

People expect me to do more than is humanly possible.

I carry with me the frailties of my age and the fetters of prejudice that are a privilege of my years.

He said this in 1997 in front of the International Olympic Committee, Lausanne, in a fruitless bid to persuade them to bring the Olympics to Cape Town in 2004.

I haven't suffered to the same extent other people have whilst I was relaxing in prison.

Any man or institution that tries to rob me of my dignity will lose.

I was not a messiah, but an ordinary man who became a leader because of extraordinary circumstances.

I seem to arrive more firmly at the conclusion that my own life struggle has had meaning only because, dimly and perhaps incoherently, it has sought to achieve the supreme objective of ensuring that each, without regard to race, colour, gender or social status, could have the possibility to reach for the skies.

On History

History shows that penalties do not deter men when their conscience is aroused.

Ordinary South Africans are determined that the past be known, the better to ensure that it is not repeated.

From a speech launching the Truth and Reconciliation Commission in February 1996.

Blaming things on the past does not make them better.

The past is a rich resource on which we can draw in order to make decisions for the future.

The purpose of studying history is not to deride human action, nor to weep over it or to hate it, but to understand it – and then to learn from it as we contemplate our future.

It is the dictate of history to bring to the fore the kind of leaders who seize the moment, who cohere the wishes and aspirations of the oppressed.

He could have been speaking about himself; he was, in fact, speaking in 1997 about the murdered black consciousness leader, Steve Bantu Biko, on the commemoration of the 20th anniversary of his death.

More often than not, an epoch creates and nurtures the individuals which are associated with its twists and turns.

On Home

I long to see the little stones on which I played as a child, the little rivers, where I swam – but I am stationed in Johannesburg.

Spoken with longing just after his release in 1990. When Nelson Mandela first built his house in the village of Qunu, Transkei, where he was brought up, he built the house identically to the one he had lived in at Victor Verster Prison, Paarl. He says he 'became friendly with the walls of the house'. To this day, he says he was happiest there, between the years 1988 and 1990.

Everybody comes back to where they were born.

He was spending Christmas 1996 at Qunu.

It becomes important, the older you get, to return to places where you have wonderful recollections.

For the years of his imprisonment, it was the modest Sowetan house he shared with his then wife, Winnie – No 8115, Orlando West – which he dreamt about. In May 1997, together with his third wife, Graça Machel, he bought a new home in Houghton, Johannesburg, specifically to make space for his twenty-one grandchildren, some of whom live with him for extended periods.

On Homosexuality

There was a time when I reacted with revulsion against the whole system of being gay.

I was ashamed of my initial views, coming from a society which did not know this type of thing.

I understand their position, and I think they are entitled to carry on with what pleases them.

On Honour

Which man of honour will desert a lifelong friend at the insistence of a common opponent and still retain a measure of credibility with his people?

From an open letter to P.W. Botha, State President of South Africa, March 1989, who had offered him a conditional freedom.

On His Hopes

As I sit in Qunu and grow as ancient as its hills, I will continue to entertain the hope that there has emerged a cadre of leaders in my own country and region, on my continent and in the world, which will not allow that any should be denied their freedom, as we were, that any should be turned into refugees, as we were, that any should be condemned to go hungry, as we were, that any should be stripped of their human dignity, as we were.

He was speaking, for the last time as South African Head of State, to the United Nations' General Assembly, New York, September 1998.

On Housing

A man is not a man until he has a house of his own.

Nelson Mandela now has several houses of his own: one is in Houghton, Johannesburg, which he shares with his partner, Graça Machel; another is in Qunu, where he spent his childhood; a third is in Cape Town. He and Graça have built another house in her native Mozambique. He also spends time in a house built for him in a game reserve, Shambala.

The families who live in shacks with no running water, sanitation, and electricity are a reminder that the past continues to haunt the present.

On Humanity

It is what we make out of what we have, not what we are given, that separates one person from another.

It is a fact of the human condition that each shall, like a meteor — a mere brief passing moment in time and space — flit across the human stage and pass out of existence.

From his address to the Joint Session of the Houses of Congress of the USA, 26 June 1990, where he was rapturously received only months after his release.

To deny any person their human rights is to challenge their very humanity.

Let the strivings of us all prove Martin Luther King, Jnr to have been correct when he said that humanity can no longer be tragically bound to the starless midnight of racism and war.

The key to the protection of any minority is to put core civil and political rights beyond the reach of temporary majorities by guaranteeing them as fundamental human rights, enshrined in a democratic constitution.

None of us can be described as having virtues or qualities that raise him or her above others.

After climbing a great hill, one only finds that there are many more hills to climb.

The universe we inhabit as human beings is becoming a common home that shows growing disrespect for the rigidities imposed on humanity by national boundaries.

Deep down in every human heart, there is mercy and generosity.

Many of us will have to pass through the valley of the shadow of death again and again before we reach the mountaintops of our desires.

On Imperialism

Imperialism means the denial of political and economic rights and the perpetual subjugation of the people by a foreign power.

Imperialism has been weighed and found wanting.

On Being Impetuous

It's very important not to shoot from the hip.

On Important Things

The important thing is to give happiness to people.

Nelson Mandela said this in a television interview to mark his eighty-fifth birthday (and the fifth anniversary of his marriage to Graça Machel).

On Inauguration Day, 10 May 1994

One of the outstanding human victories of the century.

I was overwhelmed with a sense of history.

The time for the healing of the wounds has come. The moment to bridge the chasms that divide us has come. The time to build is upon us.

Taken from his Inaugural speech. His inauguration as President of South Africa was held at the Union Buildings in Pretoria, a day no South African who watched it will ever forget.

On India

India's independence was a victory for all people under colonial rule.

A part of India's soul resides in South Africa as a revered part of our national life.

He was referring to Mahatma Gandhi.

On Islam

Islam has enriched and become part of Africa; in turn, Islam was transformed and Africa became part of it.

On Jellybeans

What are jellybeans? Are they something that is eaten?

In a Radio Good Hope interview, May 1996.

On June 16 (Youth Day)

June 16 is the day on which we South Africans commemorate the contribution of our youth to the achievement of democracy, and rededicate ourselves to creating a just society.

Celebrated in South Africa as Youth Day, June 16 1976 was the day on which the youth of Soweto rose in anger against the use of Afrikaans in schools. This escalated into what is known as the Soweto Uprising. It led directly to the end of apartheid and to the exile of many thousands of young South Africans who left the country illegally to join resistance movements such as the ANC.

On Justice

In our country and throughout the British world, as far as I know, and in the jurisprudence of many civilised countries, a person is regarded as innocent until he is convicted.

On His Last Day

On my last day I want to know that those who remain behind will say: 'The man who lies here has done his duty for his country and his people.'
On being welcomed home to Qunu on his retirement in 1999.

On Leadership

It is a mistake to think that a single individual can unite the country.

There are times when a leader can show sorrow, in public, and that it will not diminish him in the eyes of his people.
As when he comforted Nomboniso Gasa, who was raped on Robben Island in January 1997. He openly showed his distress and anger.

Many in positions of power and privilege pursue cold-hearted philosophies which terrifyingly proclaim: I am not your brother's keeper!
He was speaking to the United Nations in October 1995.

A leadership commits a crime against its own people if it hesitates to sharpen its political weapons which have become less effective.

A leader who relies on authority to solve problems is bound to come to grief.

We have the high salaries and we are living in luxury: that destroys your capacity to speak in a forthright manner and tell people to tighten their belts.

From a September 1994 interview some four months after he was inaugurated as President of South Africa.

It is important to surround yourself with strong and independent personalities, who will tell you when you are getting old.

Nelson Mandela said this in 1996 when there was speculation about his health, and queries were being raised in South Africa as to whether he would be able to complete his term of office.

It is the fate of leadership to be misunderstood; for historians, academics, writers and journalists to reflect great lives according to their own subjective canon.

The mark of great leaders is the ability to understand the context in which they are operating and act accordingly.

On Liberation

The people are their own liberators.

On Libya

The people of Libya shared the trenches with us in our struggle for freedom.

This was said at a banquet in Tripoli, Libya, in October 1997. Nelson Mandela went to great lengths to get to the pariah country, and was staunch – and even angry – in the face of American disapproval. One of his mottoes is never to forget a friend – even if they are held in opprobrium by many.

On Life

Life is like a big wheel: the one who's at the top, tomorrow is at the bottom.

On Literature

We could not have made an acquaintance through literature with human giants such as George Washington, Abraham Lincoln and Thomas Jefferson and not been moved to act as they were moved to act.

He said this in a speech to the US Congress in June 1990, shortly after his release from incarceration. One of Nelson Mandela's favourite poems was William Ernest Henley's Invictus; *Irish poet Seamus Heaney's work was also important to him, and he has quoted South African poet Ingrid Jonker on several occasions.*

When we read we are able to travel to many places, meet many people and understand the world.

Whilst on Robben Island, Mandela and his fellow prisoners avidly read Shakespeare: Coriolanus, Henry V and Julius Caesar being favourites. The prisoners staged Sophocles' Antigone, in which Mandela played the part of the tyrant Creon.

On Longevity

If your attitude is to do things which are going to please the community and human beings, then of course you are likely to live a long life. To go to bed feeling that you have done some service to the community is very important.

On Love

The world is truly round and seems to start and end with those we love.

From a letter to Winnie, 1 July 1979.

I am not nervous of love for love is very inspiring.

Spoken on his state visit to the UK, July 1996. Only a few people at that time knew of his love for Graça Machel, widow of Samora Machel, first President of Mozambique.

To be in love is an experience that every man must go through.

One should be so grateful at being involved in such an experience.

It is such a wonderful period for me.

Spoken in April 1997, and referring to his relationship with Graça Machel.

I'm in love with a remarkable lady. She has changed my life.

This was said with a broad smile in a South African television interview in February 1998. He married Graça, his third wife, on his eightieth birthday, 18 July 1998.

I don't regret the setbacks I have had before and, late in my life, I am blooming like a flower because of her support.

Again, referring to Graça Machel.

Holding Graça's hand is the one thing I love most in the world.

On Marriage

The whole purpose of a husband and wife is that when hard times knock at the door you should be able to embrace each other.

According to our custom, you marry the village and not the human being.

A man and wife usually discuss their most intimate problems in the bedroom.

Spoken in March 1996, in public, at his divorce hearing from his second wife, Winnie.

Ladies don't want to be marrying an old man like me.

On being asked towards the end of 1996 whether he would marry Graça Machel.

On His Marriage to Graça Machel, 18 July 1998

Now you won't shout at me and say I am setting a bad example.

Nelson Mandela said this to fellow Nobel Peace Prize holder, Archbishop Desmond Tutu, immediately after his marriage. Tutu had criticised him for living with Graça and setting a bad example.

My wife has put a spring in me and made me
full of hope.

He said this in May 2002 after nearly four years of marriage to Graça.

On Men

Men must follow the dictates of their conscience
irrespective of the consequences which might
overtake them for it.

On the Middle East Peace Process

The spurning of agreements reached in good
faith and the forceful occupation of land can only
fan the flames of conflict.

Extremists on all sides thrive, fed by the blood
lust of centuries gone by.

Palestinian and Israeli campaigners for peace
know that security for any nation is not abstract;
neither is it exclusive.

At the end of a century which has seen a desert
of devastation caused by horrific wars, a century
which has at last gained much experience in the

peaceful resolution of conflicts, we must ask: is this a time for war; is this a time for sending young men to their death?

This was said on his being awarded an Honourary Doctorate by Ben-Gurion University of the Negev, 19 September 1997.

On Misfortunes

There are few misfortunes in this world that you cannot turn into a personal triumph if you have the iron will and the necessary skill.

On Morality

A movement without a vision is a movement without moral foundation.

On The National Party

We are hopeful that, in their role, they will add another brick into the edifice of our young democracy.

For people that had to invoke the name of God as they made our people suffer? For people who warped the concept of Christianity to cloak the abomination of apartheid in it?

Incredulously referring to the National Party, the bulwark of apartheid until 1994, versus the South African Communist Party.

On Negotiation

Concessions are inherent in negotiations.

When you negotiate you have to accept the integrity of another man.

When you negotiate you must be prepared to compromise.

Negotiated solutions can be found even to conflicts that have come to seem intractable and that such solutions emerge when those who have been divided reach out to find the common ground.

Only free men can negotiate.

He wrote this in a letter to then State President P.W. Botha, dismissing with contempt Botha's offer of conditional release. And although it was illegal for Mandela's words to be repeated in South Africa at that time, his letter was defiantly read out to the crowds by his youngest daughter, Zindzi, at Jabulani Stadium, Soweto, on 10 February 1985. He had another five years of imprisonment to go.

On the New World Order

Can we say with confidence that it is within our reach to declare that never again shall continents, countries or communities be reduced to the smoking battlefields of contending forces of nationality, religion, race or language?

Intervention only works when the people concerned seem to be keen for peace.

If I have any moral authority – and I say if – moral authority doesn't solve world problems.

The reality can no longer be ignored that we live in an interdependent world which is bound together to a common destiny.

As the world frees itself from the dominance of bipolar power the stark division of the world's people into rich and poor comes all the more clearly into view.

We operate in a world which is searching for a better life – without the imprisonment of dogma.

Let us join hands to ensure that as we enter the new millennium, the political rights that the twentieth century has recognized, and the independence that nations have gained, shall be translated into peace, prosperity and equity for all.

As consciousness grows about the interdependence of the nations on our planet, so do all major decisions that derive from the system of governance become subject to international review and become dependent for their success on approval and support by an international constituency.

As the process of globalisation grows apace, so does the system of international governance also grow stronger.

The problems are such that for anybody with a conscience who can use whatever influence he may have to try to bring about peace, it's difficult to say no.

He was asked if, in spite of his retirement, he would help to bring about peace in Iraq (September 2002).

On the Nobel Peace Prize

Let it never be said by future generations that indifference, cynicism or selfishness made us fail to live up to the ideals of humanism which the Nobel Peace Prize encapsulates.

Nobel Peace Prize ceremony, Norway, 10 December 1993. He received the award jointly with F.W. de Klerk, at that time still State President of South Africa. The Nobel Peace Prize had a special meaning for him, because his award was preceded by two other South Africans: Chief Albert Luthuli, former president of the ANC was a Nobel Peace Prize winner, as was Archbishop Desmond Tutu.

I assumed the Nobel Committee would never consider for the peace prize the man who had started Umkhonto we Sizwe.*

"Spear of the Nation, the military wing of the ANC, formed by Nelson Mandela in June 1961. Arguing his case, he said: 'Sebatana ha se bokwe ka diatla.' ('The attacks of the wild beast cannot be averted with only bare hands.')

On Old ANC Comrades

In the last few years we have walked this road with greater frequency, marching in the procession to bid farewell to the veterans of our movement, paying our last respects to the fallen spears of the nation from a generation now reaching the end of a long and heroic struggle.

He was speaking at the funeral of his friend of 60 years, the self-effacing Walter Sisulu (May 2003).

Those of us from that generation, who are singled out to stay the longest, have to bear the pain of seeing our comrades go.

They fought a noble battle and lived their lives in pursuit of a better life for all who follow.

The democracy in which we bury them and honour them is the sweet fruit of their lives of struggle and sacrifice.

On Oppression

To overthrow oppression has been sanctioned by humanity and is the highest aspiration of every free man.

From his famous 'No Easy Walk To Freedom' speech, 1953.

For as long as legitimate bodies of opinion feel stifled, vile minds will take advantage of justifiable grievances to destroy, to kill and to maim.

I haven't suffered to the same extent other people have whilst I was relaxing in prison.

For as long as the majority of people anywhere on the continent (of Africa) feel oppressed, are not allowed democratic participation in decision-making process, and cannot elect their own leaders in free and fair elections, there will always be tension and conflict.

Never and never again shall the laws of our land rend our people apart or legalize their oppression and repression.

On The Organization of African Unity (OAU)

The midwife of our freedom.

On His Parents

My father was a polygamist with four wives and nine children.

My mother was my first friend in the proper sense of the word.

The graves mean a great deal to me because my beloved parents are here and it arouses a great deal of emotion in me because part of myself lies buried here.

He was standing next to his parents' simple graves in Qunu. His mother died while he was on Robben Island and the authorities denied him permission to attend her funeral. The first time he was able to pay his respects to her was after his release from prison in 1990.

On Peace

Peace and democracy go hand in hand.

It is not easy to talk about peace to people who are mourning every day.

I will go down on my knees to beg those who want to drag our country into bloodshed and persuade them not to do so.

Peace and prosperity, tranquillity and security are only possible if these are enjoyed by all without discrimination.

On People

I love you. You are my own flesh and blood. You are
my brothers, sisters, children and grandchildren.
Speaking to the people of South Africa.

I surely wish the pockets of my shirt were big
enough to fit all of you in.
To his compatriots in the Transkei.

Which man of honour will desert a lifelong friend
at the insistence of a common opponent and still
retain a measure of credibility with his people?
*From an open letter to P.W. Botha, State President of South Africa, March
1989, who had offered him a conditional freedom.*

Language, culture and religion are important
indicators of identity.

Justice and liberty must be our tool, prosperity
and happiness our weapon.

It is in the character of growth that we should
learn from both pleasant and unpleasant
experiences.

The suffering of the people of any single country
affects all of us no matter where we find
ourselves.

(I am) an old man who loves you all from the bottom of his heart.

You must accept the integrity of everyone and let bygones be bygones.

On Personalities

Steve Biko, murdered black consciousness activist

There can be no doubt that he was one of the most talented and colourful freedom fighters South Africa has produced.

(He was) one of the greatest sons of our nation.

That he was indeed a great man who stood head and shoulders above his peers is borne out not only by the testimony of those who knew him and worked with him, but by the fruit of his endeavours.

A fitting product of his time; a proud representative of the re-awakening of a people.

P.W. Botha, Former State President

The thing that impressed me was that he poured the tea.

After their first meeting, 4 July 1989. Mandela was still behind bars in Cape Town's Pollsmoor Prison. So unused was he to shoes with laces, that one of his captors had to tie them for him.

I will never allow him to defy the TRC.

In spite of Mandela's efforts, their tenuous relationship has curdled, with Botha's refusal, at the end of 1997, to appear before South Africa's Truth and Reconciliation Commission.

George W. Bush, President of the USA

I am aware that he is surrounded by dinosaurs who offer him all sorts of advice.

He said this as US war drums were attempting to muster support for unilateral action against Iraq, September 2002. He further separated Bush from the actions of his administration by describing Deputy President Dick Cheney as 'an arch-conservative' and George W. Bush as 'a man with whom you can do business'.

Mangosuthu Buthelezi, IFP President and Minister of Home Affairs

When we are together, he is very, very courteous. But when he is away from you, he behaves totally differently, because he does not know if he is still your friend or not.

The problem is when he leaves the cabinet and appears on public platforms. Then he behaves like any other politician.

On Prince Charles

This is a real king, not the Lion King.

Nelson Mandela's grandchildren were being introduced to Prince Charles during his historic official visit to South Africa, October 1997. The Prince of Wales was accompanied by his younger son, Prince Harry.

Bill Clinton, former US President

There is a vow of goodwill between us.

President Clinton has been my friend even before he became president. I respect him very much.

I will support my friend even if he has been deserted by the entire world.

He said this at a press conference in Washington on his last official visit to the USA as president of South Africa, September 1998.

F.W. de Klerk, former State President

He had the courage to admit that a terrible wrong had been done to our country and people through the imposition of the system of apartheid.

Despite his seemingly progressive actions, Mr de Klerk was by no means the great emancipator.

If there is anything that has cooled relations between me and Mr de Klerk, it is his paralysis as far as violence is concerned.

This was said in September 1992, with reference to the Boipatong massacre and the increasingly inexplicable 'third force' violence in South Africa.

Diana, Princess of Wales

I found her very graceful, highly intelligent, and committed to worthy causes, and I was tremendously impressed by her warmness.

(She) became a citizen of the world through her care for people everywhere.

He said this at the State Banquet for Prince Charles held in Cape Town, South Africa, on 4 November 1997.

Queen Elizabeth II

The Queen is a very gracious lady and I'm sure she'll put a country boy at ease.

On the eve of his historic – and jubilant – state visit to Britain, July 1996.

Muammar Gaddafi, President of Libya

He helped us at a time when we were all alone, when those who are now saying we should not come here were helping our enemies.

Said at the start of his controversial October 1997 visit to Libya, in the face of UN and US disapproval.

My brother leader.

Mahatma Gandhi

It would not be right to compare me to Gandhi. None of us could equal his dedication or his humility.

He showed us that it was necessary to brave imprisonment if truth and justice were to triumph over evil.

We must never lose sight of the fact that the Gandhian philosophy may be a key to human survival in the twenty-first century.

Chris Hani, assassinated leader of the ANC Youth League

A white man, full of prejudice and hate, came to our country and committed a deed so foul that our whole nation now teeters on the brink of disaster. A white women, of Afrikaner origin, risked her life so that we might know, and bring to justice, this assassin.

Speech to all South Africans, calming the angry youth after Hani's assassination at the hands of two white men (10 April 1992).

Archbishop Trevor Huddleston

His sacrifices for our freedom told us that the true relationship between our people was not one between poor citizens on the one hand and good patricians on the other, but one underwritten by our common humanity and our human capacity to touch one another's hearts across the oceans.

Ernest Urban Trevor Huddleston died in Britain in 1998 at the age of eighty-four. At his request, his ashes were brought back to South Africa, to lie in his old church in the razed suburb of Sophiatown where he worked and lived as an Anglican priest in the 1950s.

Martin Luther King, Jnr

He grappled with and died in the effort to make a contribution to the just solution of the same great issues of the day which we have had to face as South Africans.

From his Nobel Peace Prize address, 10 December 1993.

Thabo Mbeki, President of South Africa

He is polite but he is not a yes-man. He will always stand his ground.

He is a man of exceptional quality, very respectful, very warm.

He was talking about Mbeki in December 1997.

General Colin Powell, US politician

I won't wash this hand you have shaken.

It was a mutual admiration session: Colin Powell had just said: 'This is truly a very great honour for me.'

Cyril Ramaphosa, businessman

He is a son to me.

A young man of considerable ability destined to occupy a very important position in our political life.

On Walter Sisulu, politician and lifelong friend

We walked side by side through the valley of death, nursing each other's bruises, holding each other up when our steps faltered.

Nelson Mandela met Walter Sisulu in 1941. Sisulu, who died in 2003, was a singular influence on him for the rest of his life. They went to Robben Island together. The release of Sisulu ahead of his old friend was a sure sign that the unthinkable was about to happen: the release of Nelson Mandela from prison.

How can we speak about this great unifier of people without recognizing and honouring that great unity in his own life: that of Walter and Albertina as a marital couple, a unity of such deep friendship and mutual respect, a personal and political partnership that transcended and survived all hardships, separations and persecution.

On Oliver Tambo, Former President of the ANC

When I looked at him in his coffin, it was as if a part of myself had died.

Oliver Tambo was Nelson Mandela's lifelong friend. They were in law practice together. Later on the head of the ANC, Tambo lived most of his life in exile. He returned to South Africa, but died shortly afterwards, not living long enough to see his dream of a democratic South Africa realized.

He is my greatest friend and comrade for 50 years.

He enriched my own life and intellect, and neither I nor indeed this country (South Africa) can forget this colossus of our history.

On Nobel Laureate Archbishop Desmond Tutu

He's a terrific fellow.

He has been a blessing and inspiration to countless people through his ministry; his acts of compassion; his prophetic witness; and his political engagement.

Said at the thanksgiving service for the ministry of Archbishop Tutu in Cape Town, June 1996.

On Photography

Good use of photography will give even poverty with all its rags, filth and vermin a measure of divineness rarely noticeable in real life.

On Politics

Political division, based on colour, is entirely artificial and, when it disappears, so will the domination of one colour group by another.
From the dock at the Rivonia Treason Trial, 20 April 1964.

We should not allow South African politics to be relegated to trivialities chosen precisely because they salve the consciences of the rich and powerful, and conceal the plight of the poor and powerless.

If you are a politician you must be prepared to suffer for your principles.

On Poverty

It should never be that the anger of the poor should be the finger of accusation pointed at all of us because we failed to respond to the cries of the people for food, for shelter, for the dignity of the individual.

None can be at peace while others wallow in poverty and insecurity.

On Praise

I think the accolades that one gets are more because of old age.
He was eighty when he said this.

On Being President (of South Africa)

This has placed a great responsibility on my shoulders.

We enter into a covenant that we shall build a society in which all South Africans, both black and white, will be able to walk tall, without any fear in their hearts, assured of their inalienable right to human dignity – a rainbow nation at peace with itself and the world.
From his Inaugural speech, 10 May 1994.

At the end of my term I'll be eighty-one. I don't think it's wise that a robust country like South Africa should be led by a septuagenarian.

Spoken in 1996 when there were rumours about his health.

It is a way of life in which it's hard to dedicate time to the things that are really close to your heart.

My present life, even if it's not the easiest way of life, is very rewarding.

Spoken in mid 1997, one of his busiest years.

On the Press

A critical, independent and investigative press is the lifeblood of any democracy.

It was the press who never forgot us.

Spoken just after his February 1990 release.

A press conference is not a place to discuss rumours.

The press is one of the pillars of democracy.

A bad free press is preferable to a technically good, subservient one.

None of our irritations with the perceived inadequacies of the media should ever allow us to suggest even faintly that the independence of the press could be compromised or coerced.

On Prison

Nothing is more dehumanizing than isolation from human companionship.
Nelson Mandela saw Robben Island for the first time from Table Mountain, Cape Town, in 1947. Less than twenty years later, he was incarcerated there.

The long, lonely wasted years.
He was prisoner 466/64.

I believe the way in which you are treated by the prison authorities depends on your demeanour and you must fight that battle and win it on the very first day.

There I had time to just sit for hours and think.

The advantage of prison life is that you can sit and think and see yourself and your work from a distance.

In prison I had been worried by people depicting me as a superhuman being who could achieve the impossible.
He was reflecting on a long life in 1999.

On Racism

I detest racialism, because I regard it as a barbaric thing, whether it comes from a black man or a white man.

Racism pollutes the atmosphere of human relations and poisons the minds of the backward, the bigoted and the prejudiced.

Our struggle is the struggle to erase the colour line that all too often determines who is rich and who is poor.

As we enter the last decade of the twentieth century, it is intolerable and unacceptable that the cancer of racism is still eating away at the fabric of societies in different parts of our planet.

We must ensure that colour, race and gender become only a God-given gift to each one of us and not an indelible mark or attribute that accords a special status to any.

Racism is a blight on the human conscience.

We shall never again allow our country to play host to racism. Nor shall our voices be stilted if we see that another, elsewhere in the world, is victim to racial tyranny.

Racism must be consciously combated and not discreetly tolerated.

The very fact that racism degrades both the perpetrator and the victim commands that, if we are true to our commitment to protect human dignity, we fight on until victory is achieved.

All of us know how stubbornly racism can cling to the mind and how deeply it can infect the human soul.

It will perhaps come to be that we who have harboured in our country the worst example of racism since the defeat of Nazism, will make a contribution to human civilization by ordering our affairs in such a manner that we strike an effective and lasting blow against racism everywhere.

I hate the practice of race discrimination, and in my hatred I am sustained by the fact that the overwhelming majority of mankind hate it equally.

Death to racism.

Social problems don't just change because you have made a law – it takes a great deal of time.

Nelson Mandela said this in February 2004 when he was presented with an honorary doctorate from Britain's Open University by the former Speaker of the House of Commons, Baroness Betty Boothroyd.

On Reaching Heaven

I will look for a branch of the ANC and join it.

On Reconciliation

The mission of reconciliation is underpinned by what I have dedicated my life to: uplifting the most downtrodden sections of our population and all round transformation of society.

Above all the healing process involves the nation, because it is the nation itself that needs to redeem and reconstruct itself.

Reconstruction goes hand in hand with reconciliation.

We can easily be enticed to read reconciliation and fairness as meaning parity between justice and injustice.

On Regina Mundi

A church that refused to allow God's name to be used to justify discrimination and repression.

Regina Mundi is a cathedral in Soweto, frequently the focus of defiance during the struggle, and symbolic to many of the fight for freedom.

A literal battlefield between forces of democracy and those who did not hesitate to violate a place of religion with teargas, dogs and guns.

Regina Mundi became a worldwide symbol of the determination of our people to free themselves.

On Regrets

My greatest regret in life is that I never became the heavyweight boxing champion of the world.

On Relaxing

When I have no visitors over weekends, I remain the whole day in my pyjamas and eat samp.

On His Release from Prison

I greet you all in the name of peace, democracy and freedom for all.

Historic words indeed; he said them to the wildly excited crowed as he walked out of Victor Verster Prison, Paarl, holding the hand of his then wife Winnie on 11 February 1990. He was seventy-one.

I would be merely rationalizing if I told you that I am able to describe my own feelings. It was breathtaking, that is all I can say.

Along the route (from Paarl to Cape Town) I was surprised to see the number of whites who seemed to identify themselves with what is happening to the country today amongst blacks.

I was completely overwhelmed by the enthusiasm.

On Religion

Without the church, without religious institutions, I would never have been here today.

The simple lesson of religions, of all philosophies and of life itself is that, although evil may be on the rampage temporarily, the good must win the laurels in the end.

From a letter to his friend, Fatima Meer, 1 January 1976. Less than six months later, the Soweto uprising broke out, signalling the eventual end of apartheid.

The strength of inter-religious solidarity in action against apartheid, rather than mere harmony or coexistence, was critical in bringing that evil system to an end.

(African traditional religion) is no longer seen as despised superstition which had to be superseded by superior forms of belief; today its enrichment of humanity's spiritual heritage is acknowledged.

We need religious institutions to continue to be the conscience of society, a moral custodian and a fearless champion of the interests of the weak and downtrodden.

Whether you are a Christian, a Muslim, a Buddhist, a Jew or a Hindu, religion is a great force and it can help one have command of one's own morality, one's own behaviour and one's own attitude.

On His Retirement

I must step down while there are one or two people who admire me.
November 1996, when he was seventy-seven.

I intend to do a bit of farming when I step down. I will be without a job and I don't want to find myself standing at the side of the road with a placard saying: unemployed.

There is no reason whatsoever for anyone to think there will be dislocation in South Africa as a result of the stepping down of an individual.

I look forward to the period when I will be able to wake up with the sun, to walk the hills and valleys of Qunu in peace and tranquillity.
Nelson Mandela has often spoken of Qunu with longing. On this occasion it was especially so. This was the final sentence in his 'private' (as opposed to his controversial five hour 'political') speech at the historic 50th ANC conference held in Mafikeng in December 1997, when he relinquished his presidency of the ANC, and clearly looked ahead towards his retirement in 1999.

I will be able to have that opportunity in my last years to spoil my grandchildren and try in various ways to assist all South African children, especially those who have been the hapless victims of a system that did not care.

My retirement will give me the opportunity to sit down with my children and grandchildren and listen to their dreams and to help them as much as possible.

I will still go into Shell House on Mondays and carry out whatever instructions my president gives me.

Shell House, the former ANC headquarters, is in the heart of Johannesburg; his president, from mid December 1997, is Thabo Mbeki.

Born as World War I came to a close and departing from public life as the world marks half a century of the Universal Declaration of Human Rights, I have reached that part of the long walk when the opportunity is granted, as it should be to all men and women, to retire to some rest and tranquillity in the village of my birth.

Mandela was speaking to the United Nations' General Assembly in September 1998 – his last address as South African head of State. Many in the audience had tears in their eyes.

It is as a peaceful and equitable world takes

shape that I and the legions across the globe who dedicated their lives in striving for a better life for all will be able to retire in contentment and at peace.

Part of his address to the World Council of Churches, 1998.

I'll get a board that says 'Unemployed' and stand on street corners.

This was his standard joke for some time before his retirement.

I'm a part of the world. I will work with the UN, which does sterling work – if I am needed.

If there's anything that would kill me it is to wake up in the morning not knowing what to do.

He said this in 2002, when he was eighty-four.

On His Retirement as President of the African National Congress (ANC)

The time has come to hand over the baton in a relay that started more than 85 years ago in Mangaung; nay more, centuries ago when the warriors of the Autshumanyo, Makhanda, Mzilikazi, Moshweshwe, Khama, Sekkukkuni, Lobatsibeni, Cetshwayo, Nghunghunyane, Uithalder and Ramabulana, laid down their lives to defend the dignity and integrity of their being as a people.

Here are the reins of the movement – protect and guard its precious legacy.

I will remember this experience fondly for as long as I live.

I know that the love and respect that I have enjoyed is love and respect for the ANC and its ideals.

The time has come for me to take leave.

All the above quotations were taken from Nelson Mandela's valedictory address to the closing session of the historic 50th national conference of the ANC on 20 December 1997. As the speech drew to its conclusion, he had tears in his eyes.

On Revenge

You can't build a united nation on the basis of revenge.

In an interview with The New York Times *in March 1997: he was referring to the Truth and Reconciliation Commission.*

On the South African Right Wing

There are still powerful elements among whites who are not reconciled with the present transformation and who want to use every excuse to drown the country in bloodshed.

If you want to mobilize every section of the population, you can't do it with feelings of hatred and revenge.

On Robben Island

Siqithini – the Island – a place of pain and banishment for centuries, and now of triumph.

He was speaking on Heritage Day, 24 September 1997, on Robben Island itself.

Without question the harshest, most iron-fisted outpost in the South African penal system.

Robben Island, nine kilometres off the Cape coast and set in the turbulent Atlantic Ocean, has been used as a prison for hundreds of years – the first prisoner was Harry the Strandloper, confined there by the Dutch in 1658. But Robben Island is no longer a prison – it has been turned into a museum and can be visited by anyone. Mandela revisited his old prison on 11 February 1994, posing in his old cell in B Section, and showing the world the limestone quarry which he and his associates had worked in for year after year.

A symbol of the victory of the human spirit over political oppression; and of reconciliation over enforced division.

The Island has become a monument of the struggle for democracy, part of a heritage that will always inspire our children and our friends from other lands.

On the Rugby World Cup, South Africa, 1995

Our whole nation stood behind a sport which was once a symbol of apartheid.

None more so than Nelson Mandela himself. He appeared at the final wearing captain Francois Pienaar's No 6 shirt – and brought the entire country along with him, surely one of the most successful efforts at reconciliation in South Africa.

When it was 12/12 I almost collapsed. I was absolutely tense.

When I left the stadium my nerves were completely shattered.

I'm still recovering.

He said this in an interview with The New York Times *in 1997.*

On Rwanda

Rwanda stands out as a stern and severe rebuke to all of us.

The louder and more piercing the cries of despair – even when that despair results in half-a-million dead in Rwanda – the more these cries seem to encourage an instinctive reaction to raise our hands so as to close our eyes and ears.

None of us can insulate ourselves from so catastrophic a scale of human suffering.

On Sabotage

I planned it as a result of a calm and sober assessment of the situation, after many years of oppression and tyranny of my people by the whites.

From the Rivonia Treason Trial, 20 April 1964 – the trial which sent him to prison for twenty-seven years.

On Self-respect

If you are in harmony with yourself, you may

meet a lion without fear, because he respects anyone with self-confidence.

On Soccer

Soccer is one of the sporting disciplines in which Africa is rising to demonstrate her excellence, for too long latent in her womb.

On Society

The great lesson of our time is that no regime can survive if it acts above the heads of the ordinary citizens of the country.

A society that does not value its older people denies its roots and endangers its future.

On South Africa

We are marching to a new future based on a sound basis of respect.

It is in the deep interests of our country to ensure that the same principles of freedom and democracy that we hold to be true find resonance in other parts of the world.

We live with the hope that as she battles to remake herself, South Africa will be like a microcosm of the new world that is striving to be born.

Each time one of us touches the soil of this land, we feel a sense of personal renewal.

Never and never again shall it be that this beautiful land will again experience the oppression of one by another and suffer the indignity of being the skunk of the world.

From his moving Inauguration speech, 10 May 1994.

No society emerging out of the grand disaster of the apartheid system could avoid carrying the blemishes of its past.

If we are able today to speak proudly of a 'rainbow nation', it is in part because the world set us a moral example which we dared to follow.

Had the new South Africa emerged out of nothing, it would not exist.

The first founding stone of our new country is

national reconciliation and national unity. The fact that it has settled in its mortar needs no advertising.

We do face major challenges, but none are as daunting as those we have already surmounted.
On receiving the Freedom of the City of London, July 1996.

Never and never again shall the laws of our land rend our people apart or legalize their oppression and repression.

We must work for the day when we, as South Africans, see one another and interact with one another as equal human beings and as part of one nation united, rather than torn asunder, by its diversity.

Being latecomers to freedom and democracy, we have the benefit of the experience of others.

In the same way that the liberation of South Africa from apartheid was an achievement of Africa, the reconstruction and development of our country is part of the rebirth of the continent.

The hard slog of reconstruction and development is as exciting as the tremors of conflict.

South Africa is a worldwide icon of the universality of human rights; of hope, peace and reconciliation.

In time, we must bestow on South Africa the greatest gift – a more humane society.

What we have achieved will serve as a symbol of peace and reconciliation, and of hope, wherever communities and societies are in the grip of conflict.

We can never be complacent, because the legacies of our past still run very deeply through our society.

We are regarded as a pioneering nation when it comes to reaching a peaceful settlement.

On South Africans

We are all one nation in one country.

Each one of us is as intimately attached to the soil of this beautiful country as are the famous jacaranda trees of Pretoria and the mimosa trees of the bushveld.

From his Inauguration speech, 10 May 1994.

My country is rich in the minerals and gems that lie beneath its soil, but I have always known that its greatest wealth is its people, finer and truer than the purest diamonds.

It is our privilege as South Africans to be living at a time when our nation is emerging from the darkest night into the bright dawn of freedom and democracy.

Pride in our country is a common bond between us all. It is the essence of our new patriotism.

The onus is on us, through hard work, honesty and integrity, to reach for the stars.

With all our colours and races combined in one nation, we are an African people.

Having achieved our own freedom, we can fall into the trap of washing our hands of difficulties that others face.

A society for centuries trampled upon by the jackboot of inhumanity.

By joining hands South Africans have overcome problems others thought would forever haunt us.

There is no more fascinating story today than how South Africans who were enemies now work together to confound the prophets of doom who expected rivers of blood to flow.

He was speaking in Cape Town after the curtailment of his Canadian visit, September 1998, due to fatigue.

South Africans are conscious of their obligations to do whatever they can to contribute to the advancement of peace, democracy and justice whenever possible.

On Sport

Sport can reach out to people in a way which politicians can't.

I have always believed that sport is a right, not a privilege.

On The Struggle

The Struggle is my life.

From his famous press statement of 26 June 1961, whilst living underground as the Black Pimpernel.

Struggle that does not strengthen organization can lead to a blind alley.

Struggle without discipline can lead to anarchy.

Struggle without unity enables the other side to pick us off one by one.

No organization whose interests are identical with those of the toiling masses will advocate conciliation to win its demands.
From Liberation, *June 1953.*

(South Africans) displayed heroism, an incredible sense of discipline and a capacity for selflessness, as well as a quiet determination not to bend the knee to the dictates of tyrants.

The success or failure of all the campaigns against apartheid, from the 1946 African miners' strike to the resistance campaigns of the 80s, depended on a willingness to give up the comforts of life.

Running through the struggle like a golden thread is one motif – the indomitable human spirit and a moving capacity for self-sacrifice and discipline.

A willingness to make sacrifices for a loftier purpose was the unwritten code of the Struggle.

No struggle can be waged effectively in isolation.

On Survival

For me, survival is the ability to cope with difficulties, with circumstances, and to overcome them.

On Talk

Rhetoric is not important. Actions are.

On Time

Lack of punctuality is something which shows lack of respect for the organization and those appointed into positions, and a lack of self-respect.

More often than not, an epoch creates and nurtures the individuals which are associated with its twists and turns.

On Truth

No matter how hard its adversary – falsehood – may try to overwhelm it, truth refuses to yield.

I am prepared to stand by the truth even if everyone is against me.

On the Truth and Reconciliation Commission

Above all the healing process involved the nation, because it is the nation itself that needs to redeem and reconstruct itself.

The Truth and Reconciliation Commission started its work in February 1996. It heard of atrocities from the right and the left, heard testimony from murderers and torturers – and also from victims and the families of dead victims. It was intended to be an instrument of reconciliation and not of revenge.

All South Africans face the challenge of coming to terms with the past in ways which will enable us to face the future as a united nation at peace with itself.

Some criticise us when we say that whilst we can forgive, we can never forget.

Ordinary South Africans are determined that the past be known, the better to ensure that it is not repeated.

Incomplete and imperfect as the process may be, it shall leave us less burdened by the past and unshackled to pursue a glorious future.

This was said in his New Year's message to South Africa, 1998; it followed a harrowing year at the Truth and Reconciliation Commission, where the country's brutal past was opened for all to see. One of the last people called to give evidence before the Commission in 1997 was Winnie Madikizela-Mandela.

We are all bound to agonize over the price in terms of justice that the victims have to pay.

The half-truths of a lowly interrogator cannot and should not hide the culpability of the commanders and the political leaders who gave the orders.

On Ubuntu

The spirit of *Ubuntu*, that profound African sense that we are human only through the humanity of other human beings – is not a parochial phenomenon, but has added globally to our common search for a better world.

There are numerous definitions of ubuntu – kindness towards human beings is perhaps too mild; as Mandela says, it is to do with one's humanity being enriched by another's.

On Unilateral Decisions

We are really appalled by any country, whether it

be a superpower or a small country, that goes outside the United Nations and attacks independent countries.

He said this on 2 September 2002 as the USA looked increasingly unlikely to go through the United Nations in its pursuit of weapons of mass destruction in Iraq. He had also tried to phone George W. Bush himself (and failed), but had phoned George Bush Snr instead: 'I asked him to speak to his son. I have already spoken to General Colin Powell and I am waiting to speak to Condoleezza Rice. I have not given up trying to persuade President Bush not to attack Iraq.' It was also the day he awarded Nelson Mandela scholarships to 11 post-graduate students, met French President Jacques Chirac at his home, telephoned US Security Adviser Condoleezza Rice and (at 6 p.m.) launched the Fifth World Parks Congress at the Nedcor building in Sandton.

I resent any country, be it a superpower or not, that takes a unilateral decision to attack another country.

Nelson Mandela was speaking on 5 September 2002, stating at the same time that there was every reason to support the US if it attacked Iraq, providing the action had been ratified by the United Nations.

On the United Kingdom

I regard the British parliament as the most democratic institution in the world, and the independence and impartiality of its judiciary never fail to arouse my admiration.

From the Rivonia Treason Trial, 20 April 1964.

Your right to determine your own destiny was used to deny us to determine our own.

From his speech to the House of Commons, 5 May 1993.

This country has produced men and women whose names are well known in South Africa, because they, together with thousands of others of your citizens, stood up to oppose this evil system and helped to bring us to where we are today.

We return to this honoured place neither with pikes nor a desire for revenge nor even a plea to your distinguished selves to assuage our hunger for bread. We come to you as friends.

From his historic speech to both Houses of Parliament, London, 11 July 1996.

In a sense, I leave a part of my being here.

Receiving the Freedom of the City of London, July 1996.

The UK, as one of the bastions of democracy, has an obligation to ensure that we have all the material needs to entrench democracy in our country.

I love every one of you. You must understand that the people of South Africa are very grateful to you.

Addressing a crowd of 10 000 from the balcony of South Africa House, Trafalgar Square, London, July 1996.

On the USA

We are linked by nature, but proud of each other by choice.

Of New York, which he visited with Winnie on his first trip abroad after his February 1990 release, he said: 'To see it from the bottom of its great glass-and-concrete canyons while millions upon millions of pieces of ticker tape came floating down was a breathtaking experience.'

The stand you took established the understanding among the millions of our people that here we have friends, here we have fighters against racism who feel hurt because we are hurt, who seek our success because they too seek the victory of democracy over tyranny.

Address to the joint Houses of Congress of the USA, September 1994.

Let us keep our arms locked together so that we form a solid phalanx against racism.

You have felt and recognized that our success advances the very principles on which this country is founded.

How can they have the arrogance to dictate to us where we should go or who our friends should be?

A heated comment made at a dinner in Johannesburg in October 1997 on the eve of his controversial visit to Libya. The USA had expressed its disapproval of the visit.

On Violence

Government violence can do only one thing, and that is to breed counter-violence.

Take your guns, your knives and your pangas, and throw them into the sea.
His first speech in the troubled province of KwaZulu-Natal after his release from prison, 25 February 1990.

People who kill children are no better than animals.

Use violence only in self-defence.

In the end, the cries of the infant who dies because of hunger or because a machete has slit open its stomach, will penetrate the noises of the modern city and its sealed windows to say: am I not human too!
From his historic speech to both Houses of Parliament of the United Kingdom, 11 July 1996.

We hope the world will reach a stage when it realizes that the use of violence against any community is something that puts us next to animals.

Violence and non-violence are not mutually exclusive; it is the predominance of the one or the other that labels a struggle.

On The Vote

The question of education has nothing to do with the question of the vote.

As in Zimbabwe, there was a vocal section of white voters who maintained that the vote should not be given to uneducated or barely literate people. Some form of qualification, resulting in a limited franchise, was suggested. This was rejected – as it had been in Zimbabwe – in favour of one man, one vote.

A vote without food, shelter and health care would be to create the appearance of equality while actual inequality is entrenched.

On White South Africans

The majority of white men regard it as the destiny of the white race to dominate the man of colour.

From the ANC Youth League Manifesto of 1944, largely written by him.

White supremacy implies black inferiority.

From the dock at the Rivonia Treason Trial, 20 April 1964.

Just as many whites have killed just as many blacks.

Asked about deaths of white civilians in ANC attacks, 1990.

Whites fear the reality of democracy.

As long as whites think in terms of group rights they are talking the language of apartheid.

Spoken before the April 1994 elections.

Whites are fellow South Africans and we want them to feel safe, and we appreciate the contribution they have made towards the development of this country.

They have had education, they have got the knowledge, skills and expertise. We want that knowledge and expertise now that we are building our country.

The whites still think as if there were no blacks, or coloureds, or Indians.

Said on his wildly successful state visit to the United Kingdom, July 1996.

On Winnie

I had hoped to build you a refuge, no matter how small, so that we would have a place for rest and

sustenance before the arrival of the sad, dry days.
From a letter to Winnie from Robben Island, 26 June 1977.

Had it not been for your visits, wonderful letters and your love, I would have fallen apart many years ago.
From a letter to Winnie, 6 May 1979.

I have often wondered whether any kind of commitment can ever be sufficient excuse for abandoning a young and inexperienced woman in a pitiless desert.
Letter to Winnie after her 1986 'boxes of matches' speech.

I am convinced that your pain and suffering was far greater than my own.
From his first speech as a free man, Cape Town, 11 February 1990.

I cannot say for certain if there is such a thing as love at first sight, but I do know that the moment I first glimpsed Winnie Nomzamo, I knew that I wanted to have her as my wife.
They were married on 15 June 1958.

She married a man who soon left her; that man became a myth; and then that myth returned home and proved to be just a man after all.
In a curiously similar turn of phrase, Graça Machel, widow of President Samora Machel of Mozambique, and Nelson Mandela's third wife, said of him in an interview at the beginning of 1998: 'I found this very simple man who appeared so humble, so soft, so common. It was a conflict between myth and the reality.'

I embrace her with all the love and affection I have nursed for her inside and outside prison from the moment I first met her.

Announcing his separation from Winnie, 13 April 1992.

My love for her remains undiminished.

Part of his poignant separation announcement.

I was the loneliest man during the period I stayed with her.

During his divorce trial, March 1996.

On Women

The beauty of a woman lies as much in her face as in her body.

From a letter to his daughter Zindzi, 5 March 1978.

If a pretty woman walks by, I don't want to be out of the running.

He was talking to foreign correspondent Patti Waldmeir at the time.

Women today are very sensitive to men expressing opinions without consulting them. Freedom cannot be achieved unless women have been emancipated from all forms of oppression.

It's a unique woman who can turn the whole

world around and make it the best living place to experience.

Nelson Mandela said this in May 2002, some four years after his marriage to Graça Machel.

On Work

Job, jobs and jobs are the dividing line in many families between a decent life and a wretched existence.

Workers need a living wage – and the right to join unions of their own choice and to participate in determining policies that affect their lives.

On Writing

Writing is a prestigious profession which puts one right into the centre of the world and, to remain on top, one has to work really hard, the aim being a good and original theme, simplicity in expression and the use of the irreplaceable word.

From a letter to his daughter Zindzi, 4 September 1977.

On Youth

I admire young people who are concerned with the affairs of their community and nation perhaps because I also became involved in struggle whist I was still at school.

Young people are capable, when aroused, of bringing down the towers of oppression and raising the banners of freedom.

I appeal to the youth and all those on the ground: start talking to each other across divisions of race and political organizations.

I pay tribute to the endless heroism of youth.

Whenever I am with energetic young people, I feel like a recharged battery.

On Zulus

No people can boast more proudly of having ploughed a significant field in the Struggle.

The Battle of Isandlwana in 1879 has been an inspiration for those of us engaged in the struggle for justice and freedom in South Africa.

The battle took place under a midday eclipse on 22 January 1879.

When my sentence has been completed I will still be moved, as men are always moved, by their consciences; I will still be moved by my dislike of the race discrimination against my people when I come out from serving my sentence, to take up again, as best I can, the struggle for the removal of those injustices until they are finally abolished once and for all.

Spoken in court, on 7 November 1962, at the end of the Old Synagogue Trial, when he was convicted and sentenced to three year's imprisonment on charges of incitement and two year's imprisonment for leaving South Africa without valid travel documents.

Sources

ANC Youth League Manifesto, 1944; BBC; *The Citizen*; *Leadership*; *Liberation* (June 1953); M-Net *(Funigalore)*; *Saturday Star*; *The Star*; *Sunday Times*; *Mail & Guardian*; *Sowetan*; *The Argus*; *Cape Times*; SAPA; AP; *Business Day*; *Newsweek*; Reuters; *RSA Review 1995*; *The Natal Witness*; *Vogue* (French edition), Dec 1993/Jan 1994; *Time*; *The New York Times*; *The Financial Times*; *The Daily Telegraph*; *The Sunday Telegraph*; *The Sunday Independent*; *ThisDay*

The Struggle is My Life (Pathfinder, New York); *Nelson Mandela: The Man and the Movement* by Mary Benson (Penguin); *Higher than Hope* by Fatima Meer (Skotaville); *The Historic Speech of Nelson Rolihlahla Mandela at the Rivonia Trial* (Learn & Teach Publications); *Rivonia – Operation Mayibuye: A Review of the Rivonia Trial* by HHW de Villiers (Afrikaanse Pers-Boekhandel); *Anatomy of a Miracle* by Patti Waldmeir (WW Norton & Company, 1997); *Madiba* (Martin Schneider), 1997; *Beyond the Miracle* by Allister Sparks (Jonathan Ball Publishers)

Radio Good Hope; Radio 702; SABC; SATV (Allister Sparks' interview) 1998; Carte Blanche (M-Net) 2004; ANC Youth League Manifesto, 1944;

No Easy Walk to Freedom speech, 21.9.1953; A New Menace in Africa speech, March 1958; Verwoerd's Tribalism speech, May 1959; The Struggle is My Life press statement, 26.6.1961; Letter to the Prime Minister, Dr HF Verwoerd, 26.6.1961; Address to the Conference of the Pan-African Freedom Movement of East and South Africa, Addis Ababa, January 1962; Black Man in a White Court Trial speech, the Old Synagogue, Pretoria, 7.11.1962; Rivonia Treason Trial speech, 20.4.1964; Letter to his daughter Zindzi Mandela, 4.9.1977; Mandela's Call to the Youth of South Africa smuggled speech, 1980; Whilst Still in Prison, his first speech in almost 25 years, defiantly read by Zindzi Mandela, 10.2.1985; Release from Victor Verster Prison speech, Cape Town, 11.2.1990; Bishopscourt press conference, 12.2.1990; FNB Stadium (Soccer City) speech, Johannesburg 13.2.1990; Bloemfontein speech, 25.2.1990; Durban Rally speech, 25.2.1990; Address to the Swedish Parliament, 13.3.1990; Harlem speech, New York, 21.6.1990; Address to the Joint Session of the Houses of Congress of the USA, 26.6.1990; Announcement of his separation from Winnie, 13.4.1992; Gandhi Hall, Lenasia, speech, 27.9.1992; Speech to the House of Commons, United Kingdom, 5.5.1993; Acceptance Address at the Clark University Investiture,

Atlanta, 10.7.1993; Nobel Peace Prize Award Ceremony speech, Oslo, Norway, 10.12.1993; ANC Election Victory speech, 2.5.1994; Inauguration speech, 10.5.1994; Address to the 49th Session of the General Assembly, United Nations, 3.10.1994; Business Leaders speech, New Delhi, India, 26.1.1995; African Cup of Nations Tournament speech, 13.1.1996; Opening of SA Parliament speech, 9.2.1996; Interfaith Commissioning Service for the Truth & Reconciliation Commission speech,13.2.1996; University of Potchefstroom speech, 19.2.1996; Thanksgiving Service for the Ministry of Archbishop Tutu, Cape Town, 23.6.1996; SA Representatives to Olympic & Paralympic Games, Atlanta, speech, 28.6.1996; Freedom of the City of London, Guildhall speech, 10.7.1996; Joint Houses of Parliament Speech, London, 11.7.1996; OAU Summit speech, Yaounde, 8.7.1996; Bastille Day speech, Paris, 14.7.1996; 75th Anniversary of the South African Communist Party speech, 28.7.1996; Warrenton Presidential School Project speech, 30.8.1996; Signing of the SA Constitution speech, Sharpeville 10.12.1996; Food for Life, Pietermaritzburg speech, 23.4.1997; Freedom of Pietermaritzburg speech, 25.4.1997; State Banquet speech for President Museveni of Uganda, 27.5.1997; Lecture at the Oxford Centre for Islamic Studies, 11.7.1997; Commemoration of the 20th Anniversary of Steve Biko's Death speech, East London 12.9.1997; Honorary Doctorate by Ben-Gurion University of the Negev, Cape Town, 19.9.1997; Heritage Day speech, Robben Island, 24.9.1997; State Banquet for Prime Minister Gujral of India, Cape Town 7.10.1997; Collar of the Nile Speech, Cairo, 21.10.1997; Colonel Qadhafi speech, Tripoli, 22.10.1997; Presentation of the Africa Peace Award to Mozambique, Durban, 1.11.1997; State Banquet for Prince Charles speech, Cape Town, 4.11.1997; Foreign Correspondents Association speech, Johannesburg, 21.11.1997; Freedom of the City of Cape Town speech, 27.11.1997; Bram Fischer Memorial Trust speech, Bloemfontein, 28.11.1997; Regina Mundi Day speech, Soweto, 30.11.1997; International Day of Solidarity with the Palestinian People speech, Pretoria, 4.12.1997; Farewell as President of the ANC speech, Mafikeng, 20.12.1997; OAU Heads of State & Government speech, Ouagadougou, Burkina Faso, 8.6.1998; Freedom of the City of Cardiff speech, Cardiff, Wales, 16.6.1998; Sowetan Nation Building 10th Anniversary speech, Johannesburg, 30.6.1998; Chris Hani Award speech, 10th National Congress of the South African Communist Party, Johannesburg, 1.7.1998; Closing ceremony speech at the 19th Meeting of Heads of Government of the Caribbean Community, St Lucia, 4.7.1998; State Banquet for President Rawlings of Ghana speech, Pretoria, 9.7.1998; Aids Speech, Paris, 14.7.2003; International Year of Older Persons speech, Cape Town, 17.7.2003; 46664 Give One Minute of Your Life to Aids speech, 21.10.2003